pantomime: elements and exercises

pantomime:

THE UNIVERSITY PRESS OF KANSAS / LAWRENCE / MANHATTAN / WICHITA

elements and exercises

by David Alberts

photographs by C. James Gleason

Grateful acknowledgment for help
in the preparation of this book is accorded
Nancy Wynn Zucchero
Cherelaine
William A. Moses
and
Elaine Robinson

contents

introduction

The art of mime is outside or rather beyond all instinct. To develop it, one must do all the supple and strong exercises; the mind must be constantly awake and aware; one needs a good will without defiance or weakness, and an ideal in one's heart.
— Étienne Decroux

In 1923 Étienne Decroux undertook his study of the various aspects of mime that could be learned and practiced by actors. While a student at the École du Vieux-Columbier in Paris he stylized the expression of the body through movement and gesture, taking into consideration the action, speed, and intensity of all possible body movements. He later defined their meaning, in rational and abstract ideas, as a basis for all articulate and distinct movements, thereby establishing the foundation for the "modern" school of the art of pantomime.

Decroux was very much concerned with clarity and accuracy in form and movement. He originated a repertory of physical expression, the *Mime Statuaire* or *Mime Subjectif,* and also formed the *Mime Objectif,* a concept of illusion through which the performer can represent concrete objects by exact suggestive movements coupled with imagination.

As a professor at Charles Dullin's School of Dramatic Art, and having founded the Théâtre de Mime Français, Decroux was able to teach his newly innovated art form to others. One of his first students, Jean Louis Barrault, became his colleague, and together they advanced the art through study and performance. Barrault subsequently devoted his talents to the spoken theatre, and formed the Compagnie Madeleine Renaud–Jean Louis Barrault at the Marigny Theatre in 1946.

Barrault produced four mime plays there, one of which, "Baptiste"—adapted from the film *Les Enfants du Paradis*—helped to enhance the career of another student of Decroux, Marcel Marceau, who is perhaps the most widely known pantomimist in the history of the art. Marceau developed his own repertoire of "style" exercises, those exemplifying a highly advanced technical ability, and pantomimes based on the teachings of Decroux, the works of Decroux and Barrault, and the principle of pantomime as "total theatre." It is from the fundamentals of Decroux, Barrault, and Marceau that the exercises and elements contained in these pages are derived.

As pantomime is not only a pure art form but also an underlying element in many of the performing arts, this book was written in an effort to provide actors, dancers, aspiring pantomimists, and others with an introduction and guide to the specialized exercises and essential physical elements of the art of pantomime. It is not intended as an alternative to a qualified teacher of pantomime, but as an introduction and guide, and as a necessary link between the mental concepts of the art, such as creativity and style, and the actual physical performance.

part one:

elements

INTRODUCTION TO THE ELEMENTS

The principle elements of pantomime, *essence* and *illusion,* are so closely related as to be, at times, indistinguishable from one another: The essence of illusion is illusion of the essence, the illusion of which . . . and so on. Suffice it to say that neither can be satisfactorily explained independent of the other, although an attempt has been made to differentiate the two where possible.

The mental concepts of essence and illusion are nonetheless applicable to physical performance, through delineation, imitation, and the illusory exercises which are included in Part Two.

ESSENCE

Pantomime, as an art form, is fundamentally concerned with the communication of experiences. An experience, in this context, is any object, action, situation, or event, real or imaginary, which is consciously encountered, either subjectively or objectively, by observation or direct participation. Each experience is unique in its relation to every other experience.

Certain characteristics of each experience have been abstracted as representative, or symbolic, of the entire experience, the significance of each characteristic having been determined by convention, or conventional standards. Convention is, itself, a comprehensive system of abstractions. It consists of intelligible and self-explanatory signs and symbols, composed of one or more abstractions, through which experiences are reduced to their general outlines and/or predominant characteristics. The most highly developed system of symbolic reference which mankind has evolved is the spoken language. By means of language we can conceive of intangibles such as ideas, thoughts, and emotions, as well as elements of the perceptual world usually attributed to reality. Through language we can describe, imagine, reason, remember, think, and above all, communicate.

In pantomime, since the communication of experiences can only be expressed in terms of physical action, there is considerable reliance upon abstraction and convention, in the physical sense. Abstraction permits a representation of experiences simply, clearly, and rapidly; convention helps to determine the delineation of the experience defined; both abstraction and convention condense experiences into units simple enough to be comprehended one at a time. This abstract, sequential representation is totally compatible with our own abstract, sequential comprehension. The human mind does not possess the ability to comprehend or conceive more than one idea at a time. Communication must then, of necessity, progress along the lines of least resistance. Abstraction and convention offer the least resistant means of communication, and the most reliable. Communication by abstraction-convention allows translation of a universe in which all experiences occur simultaneously, a universe which defies perfect description in abstract, physical expression. The perfect description of even a solitary experience would take an interminable length of time. As a result, each experience is interpreted in pantomime in terms of its fundamental, distinguishable, abstracted, physically delineable characteristic—its essence.

Essence is a product of the mind, of "awareness," association, and thought.

Awareness is the key. Through awareness, the unique characteristic of each experience is discerned and, by association, maintained. The power of thought enables us to construct a symbol, or symbols, of each experience, apart from the experience itself. Because the idea is more substantial to the mind than the reality, the symbol is therefore more intelligible than the fact.

ILLUSION

Pantomime does not exist in reality, but exists in imagination to the very limits of reality.

Illusion is directly contingent upon perception—perception in the sense of what is visualized, not necessarily that which actually exists. Generally speaking, any visual perception which is incongruous with physical measurement may be termed an illusion. However, physical measurement of objects and space fail to provide a reliable description of what is, or should be, perceived. Perception is determined as much by the nature of the mind as by any external influences upon the senses. The mind does not necessarily perceive things as they are or as they are in relation to each other; that is, the mind does not consistently interpret the impressions of the senses correctly. Lines, areas, and masses, for example, as well as size and distance, are relative, and are not always perceived in their actual physical relationship. An average-size person will appear tall or short, depending upon his relationship to the surrounding environment. Perceptual judgment is constantly influenced by prior experiences and present expectations. People rarely see all there is to be seen, or recall what was seen accurately. There is a definite tendency to "fill in the blanks" in the perception, based on an expectation of what would be appropriate to be seen. On the basis of the significance of an experience, an assumption is made that the perception of certain sensations or impressions will fulfill the level of experience desired. Experience and expectation determine the significance attached to the visualization, and also set a standard for the inferences, or judgments made concerning the perception. These judgments are often made spontaneously, the resulting visualization being primarily subconscious. Conse-

quently, a few of our perceptions, or *conceptions*, are entirely complete or adequate. Only a part of what is perceived comes through the senses; the remainder emanates from within.

Enter the pantomimist. He deals not only with simple physical illusions, such as walking or climbing stairs, but also with the concept of illusory illusions—the delineation and usage of imaginary objects which do not exist in "reality"; tangible intangibles which exist only in the mind. The pantomimist must present an illusion of reality which is, for the most part, an illusion itself. During the course of a performance he will describe situations, delineate objects, and portray characters, all in imagination, presenting a myriad of physical-visual-mental illusions for the purpose of ascribing them to reality.

This presentation usually takes form in a void—a bare, soundless stage. The void, then, is in no way different from the characteristics of the form; conversely, what is perceived as form, or formal characteristics, is really the void. Time and space are likewise synthesized. There is no other time than the present—past and future are simply grammatical abstractions. Space is no longer a reality of the physical world, but a means by which we perceive experiences apart from one another. The concepts of time and space become arbitrary in the sense that each is expanded or condensed to suit the needs of the performer. There is a return to nothingness, or emptiness, the value of which lies in the movement it permits and in the substance, real or imaginary, which it differentiates and contains. But the emptiness must come first. The mind must be liberated from the restrictive concepts of time, space, reality, and like abstractions. The performer is then free to function spontaneously in the void. When the collective mind of the audience is likewise unencumbered, it is readily accessible and highly receptive to ideas, sensations, and illusions impressed upon it.

There is one discernible difference between the perception of a "reality" and of an "illusion." Once the sensations or impressions of either a reality or an illusion have been assembled in the mind, there is still recognition of a relationship between the sense-impressions and supplementary influences. But the main factor governing the perception-visualization of illusion, more than the perception of reality, is imagination. The visualizing ability of an audience increases in direct proportion to the stimulation of the imagination, to a point at which illusion and reality, in the conventional sense, are synonymous.

Imagination may apply to a mental representation (image) either of what is remembered, of what has never been experienced in its entirety, or of what is actually nonexistent. By altering or rearranging the elements of reality, the pantomime performer provides an image of something not present to the senses, something which could exist, but in fact does not. The "elements of reality" in pantomime, however, are limited to the performer himself. As a result, pantomime is nearly as dependent upon the audience for its meaning and interpretation as the audience is upon the performer. The audience must supply that which the performer is unable to supply—responsive imagination. It is insufficient for a member of an audience simply to sit and watch interesting movement patterns. He must respond with his imagination to the ideas presented to him through movement and gesture, since what he "sees" is motivated as much by himself as by any external influence.

The main concern in the performance of pantomime is the presentation of the subject matter within the framework of the plot. The emphasis is on the accurate delineation of objects, settings, situations, and/or characters, and other elements of the pantomime. The responsive imagination of the audience is centered in this area of delineation. The audience need only be aware of the description of these elements for a relatively thorough understanding of the performance. Pantomime, being explicit, is least vulnerable to undesired variance in interpretation, but quite vulnerable in the case of a member of an audience who is unfamiliar with the conventions of the stage or of pantomime. The performer's technical ability then becomes a definite factor in the understanding of a performance. The better the performer, the greater will be the imaginative response. And since the audience readily comprehends its own responses, the better will be the understanding.

To be effective, a pantomime must progress smoothly and rapidly; to dwell on any particular movement or gesture, unless for effect, lends a different meaning, or no meaning, to a performance, and tends to distract from the overall impression. A good pantomime leaves little to question in the mind of the audience. It progresses simply and clearly to its culmination. Any illusion intended to stimulate the imaginative response of the audience must also progress simply and clearly, smoothly and rapidly. Nothing will disrupt the concentration and response of an audience more than an illusion which is ill-conceived, ill-timed, poorly executed, or extraneous. Illusions, although calculated and contrived, must seem natural phenomena which take place unobtrusively throughout a performance.

DELINEATION

To delineate any object in imagination, it is necessary to rely upon some physical means of communication as to what each object is, what it is used for, and the meaning derived from that use. Delineation is

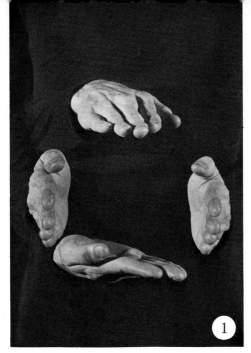

the most integral part, the vocabulary, of the physical performance of pantomime. The importance of accurate and controlled delineation is obvious. Exposition in pantomime selections (usually called "sketches") is devoted almost entirely to delineation. It is through delineation that communication of experiences can be expressed.

The study of delineation begins with an understanding of the physical qualities, or characteristics, of objects, and the level(s) of perception attributed to each. In pantomime, *outline-form* and *surface-content* are the first items of delineation, and the most perceptible. Outline-form and surface-content consist of the overall dimensions, shape, texture, and the number of related objects, or parts of objects. Delineation of this is accomplished by inscribing in the air an accurate outline of the object, and by defining any notable characteristics or peculiarities in this outline or on the surface of the object. Very little movement is required for well-known objects; a minimum outline will suffice *(Figure 1)*. The more complex the object, the more attention need be paid to delineation on this level, allowing for complete comprehension

by every member of the audience. An audience which is confused at the outset can progress no further.

The second level, *solid-form* delineation, is more complex than outline-form, and therefore more liable to error, not only in the delineation, but in perception as well. Solid-form delineation includes the characteristics of weight, or mass, and all previously assigned characteristics. Every object delineated in pantomime must have weight, and this weight must be accurate and applicable to the situation. But since imaginary objects have no real weight, imaginary weight is artificially defined. The illusion of weight is achieved by muscular compensation—an accurate bodily reaction to the supposed weight of an object *(Figure 2)*. The muscular compensation for the weight of an imaginary box, for instance, is a step in the delineation of what may be inside the box, if anything.

Also included in the second level of delineation is the characteristic of *motion,* defined as any activity involving an object which is not a product of the object itself. In the pulling of a rope *(Figure 3)* there is a definite bodily reaction to a stress exerted,

7

3

not by the rope, but by some unseen, external force acting upon the rope and, subsequently, upon the performer.

Most delineation is expressed on these two levels. Characteristics assigned are referred to, for purposes of pantomime, as *primary qualities*. In other words, dimensions, motion, number, weight, shape, texture, and inherent physical abilities of any object are considered primary qualities.

The next level of delineation-perception involves the elemental visual perceptions of light, intensity, and color. From a purely visual standpoint, light of a sufficient intensity is absolutely essential for perception. This is also true in pantomime, except that the perception of the performer is the only necessity. The element of light is taken for granted unless the performer specifically alters the situation. Intensity is also understood, except in the delineation of objects which produce their own light, such as the sun, light bulbs, and other luminous entities, in which case the intensity is defined by a reaction to the supposed brightness of the light emitted. Delineation of color is difficult to express conclusively in pantomime, and should be dismissed as

impractical, not simply because it is difficult, but because each member of an audience will assign a color to each object delineated based on his own interpretation of the delineation, regardless of the performer's intentions. In any event, color is of little consequence to objects which don't exist.

The other sense-oriented qualities of *taste, smell,* and *sound* compose the final level of delineation-perception. Taste and smell can be expressed only in generalities, usually in terms of good-bad, sweet-sour, pleasant-unpleasant, and so on. The delineation of sound is, for all practical purposes, irrelevant and impossible. We can define "listening," "hearing," or related reactions, but not "sound." First of all, imaginary objects make no sound, and since all qualities expressed in pantomime must be defined in terms of physical action, not simply in thought, an audience can neither perceive nor comprehend what may be present in the performer's mind unless the sound itself is present. The question of sound effects arises at this point. In the purist tradition, sound effects have no place in the pursuit of the pantomime illusion.

8

The last two levels of delineation include the *secondary qualities* of light, intensity, color, taste, smell, and sound—irrelevant or otherwise. These secondary characteristics involve more of an empathy than an actual delineation since none can be positively defined, even in context. Primary qualities are relatively stable, but secondary qualities are dependent upon too many factors, including the performer and the individuality of each member of the audience to allow any comprehensive or "standard" interpretation.

Primary and secondary qualities are generally interdependent. In pantomime, however, these qualities need not be united in time and space, as they must be in nature. (This is within the concept of arbitrary time and space.) The delineating characteristics of an apple, for example, lie only in primary qualities—dimensions (roundness), edibility, and "shine-ability." The secondary qualities of the object are not relevant to this definition. In most cases, secondary qualities can only be expressed *after* definition and tentative recognition of an object, even those highly dependent upon secondary qualities for

clearest delineation.

In simplest terms, the physical approach to delineation is as follows: each performer should feel, handle, and use as many objects as are available to him, remembering the physical sensations attributed to each. He should then express the object, without the object itself, in any way necessary to convey its physical characteristics as simply, clearly, accurately, deliberately, and quickly as possible. Following this delineation is the handling of the object, in imagination, retaining all delineated qualities.

The following is an outline of an exercise in which the main objective is the recognition and delineation of primary qualities. It is elementary in concept and allows for considerable variation.

1. Look at the object. Where is it located in relation to its surroundings? In how much space does it rest?

2. Grasp the object, one or both hands. How was the object approached? Take into consideration the entire body, then arm, hand, and fingers in particular. What are the object's

dimensions? In what position are the arm, hand, fingers, and body in an attempt to move the object?

3. Pick up the object. How heavy is it? What are the muscular compensations for its weight? Note any changes in the position of the arm, hand, and fingers from #2.

4. Handle the object. What are the physical reactions to the movement of the object? These reactions are very complex, particularly in the areas of muscular compensation and timing. The reactions involve not only the body as a whole, but also a continuous eye contact with the object.

5. The object should now be used in its primary function, then in any and all functions possible, no matter how unlikely. Again, retain an awareness of all reactions, compensations, and timing involved.

6. Repeat steps 1 through 5, until all aspects of the object are firmly fixed in mind and body. A single progression through these steps is insufficient.

7. When all characteristics of the object have been fairly well established, decide which one physically delineable characteristic distinguishes this object from any other. This may involve either a single movement, or a combination of closely related movements, and will determine the essence of the object, at least on the primary level.

The next step is to form an illusion of the object without utilizing the object itself in any way. The simplest way is to duplicate, exactly, every movement that was made throughout the preceding exercise, imagining the object continuously, with these points in mind: (1) All objects delineated in pantomime must have an *origin*. By origin is meant the exact point in arbitrary time and space at which an object exists. This is the point from which delineation begins. Origin must be clear and precise, but not overly obvious. (2) From origin, each object must retain all qualities assigned and understood, unless intentionally and specifically altered. An audience remembers most, if not all characteristics delineated, particularly the size and placement of objects in relation to the performer. (3) Objects defined must be acted upon, or used, by the performer. Essence can only be expressed in usage, or function, through delineation. The shining of an imaginary apple distinguishes this object from any other round, edible object and delineates it far more clearly than by any other means. Any object delineated without origin or function lends no meaning to a performance and serves only to clutter up the performing area with unusable, unrelated distraction. Every object must commence existence in delineation and serve a useful, intelligible purpose.

At times, a simple duplication of the preceding exercise will prove unsuccessful in rapid or clear delineation of the object in question. This necessitates a refining process in which all movement extraneous to the delineation is eliminated. This will entail, in some instances: (1) an exaggeration of a particular characteristic, usually the essence; (2) a distortion of timing or muscular compensation involving the object; (3) a subtle repetition of any possibly confusing material already expressed, or; (4) all the above, leaving only the clearest,

simplest, quickest, and most accurate definition of the object.

Other means of delineation, dependent upon the level of perception, comprehension, or expediency:

Functional delineation: Some objects are delineated by their function, more so than by their initial primary or secondary quality delineation. A broom, for example, is not a very distinguishable object until it is used. Its function is its delineation, and vice versa. This is not to say that some objects need not be delineated; however, once an origin has been established for any primarily functional object, only a brief definition of dimensions is necessary before proceeding to the object's function.

Personification: Part of the body, usually the arm, hand, or fingers becomes an object, while the rest of the body retains its own identity, or one previously assumed. Books, flowers, snakes, butterflies, and other objects, mostly animate, are delineated in this manner.

Delayed revelation: A significant or qualifying characteristic of an object is withheld, then replaced at the performer's discretion, to effect a surprise ending, or to explore the implications of the object's origin, delineation, or function.

There are, of course, many objects unfamiliar to one or more members of an audience. The handling and function of any such object should dispel this confusion. If all else fails, it may prove advantageous to incorporate the name of the object into the title of the pantomime sketch. Individual experience and experimentation will best determine the course of action. In addition, there are numerous conventions used in all areas of delineation. Some are simple, some complex, each built upon tradition, evolution, and conventions of the stage. A good teacher of pantomime should be sought for an explanation and demonstration of these conventions.

It is apparent that no two performers will experience the same sensations in the delineation and handling of real and imaginary objects. The ideas expressed are therefore entirely subjective, intended as guidelines rather than rules of order, and should be related to each performer's approach to the material, modified in accordance with individual means of expression and interpretation.

IMITATION

Imitation is primarily an exercise in perception, coordination, and artificial characterization. Imitation and characterization, although closely related, are not the same procedurally. Characterization is a subjective, personal combination of mimicry, creativity, and imagination, whereas imitation is simply objective mimicry, controlled and detailed, without implication. Through selective imitation, creativity and imagination form characterization. The study of imitation provides for more substantial, realistic and, most important, believable characterization. Imitation-mimicry in pantomime is not a cursory examination and surface representation of individuals, particularly those with eccentric movements or physical peculiarities. It is a detailed study of "people, places, and things," each in relation to the other.

There is no set procedure of imitation. The best approach is to study, in detail, people of varying age, sex, background, and occupation, and their means of expression, habits, stance, gestures, movements, reactions to, and handling of objects and situations, in relation to themselves and to others; then to duplicate, as accurately as possible, every action and reaction observed. The analysis must be objective. Often there is a tendency to project oneself, either mentally or physically, into the study. This is not necessarily detrimental in characterization, but should be avoided in imitation. The more objective the analysis, the more accurate the imitation. (In this sense, imitation of plants and animals does serve a useful purpose. By studying the movement of non-human elements in nature, analysis is placed in proper perspective, and projection of subjective human characteristics is limited.) The next step in characterization would be to disregard any aspect(s) of the analysis considered superfluous or irrelevant. This may occur to some extent in imitation, but is due to personal, physical limitations, not subjective elimination. All aspects of any imitation should be retained intact for future duplication in characterization.

One guideline may prove helpful in analysis and imitation. There are basically two types of physical actions—voluntary and involuntary. Involuntary actions are those which occur automatically to the individual, with little or no forethought—everyday movements, gestures, unconscious mannerisms, reflex actions. Voluntary actions are those which require a thoughtful, deliberate, and controlled action for a specific purpose, such as social and occupational movements and gestures. Voluntary actions are the most obvious. Involuntary actions are less discernible since they have been thoroughly ingrained in the individual, and are the foundation of his physical character.

"Character," says Plutarch, "is simply habit long continued." The physical and mental character of any individual is composed of numerous recurrent actions and reactions, both voluntary and involuntary, any one of which could be the basis for a considerably complex characterization. The objective is to be aware of all possible body functions, for a given character in a given situation, and be able to duplicate each function accurately, within physical limitations.

CLOSING NOTES, PART ONE

Pantomime is an individual art. This

is of necessity. The essence of the art is in the communication between one individual and another, by movement and gesture, not in terms of speed and distance, but in terms of understanding and experience. An artist need not be necessarily aloof, but must be vigorously independent. In a society in which teamwork is the stronghold of mediocrity—mass-production, mass-media enforce it, mass-education insures it—pantomime remains an art limited to those who have the determination to pursue a discipline which has little regard for politics, economics, or statistics, except as curious subject matter. The art of silence must speak clearly, not dogmatically or hypocritically.

The ideal is solo performance. The performer alone is at the same time master and foil of the universe, a universe which he fashions in accordance with its own dictates. So much for poetic sustenance. The reality of the matter is that there are few opportunities for solo performers outside the educational environment. Pantomime companies offer a more likely, yet not overly abundant, opportunity for performance. The experience of working with and learning from others, the exchange of ideas, methods, and philosophies is invaluable. A few notes on group performances: The communicative ability of an individual performer decreases as the number of performers increases. This should be taken into consideration when attempting group pieces. Not as much can be said as in solo performance because the concentration and response of the audience is more widespread. Concerning "mimodramas," "mimeplays," and the like, if costumes, sets, and various special effects are provided in performance, there seems to be little point in withholding speech. A minimum is left to the imagination of the audience, a slight to their imaginative ability in the first place, and a presumptuous assertion by the performer(s) in the second. Likewise, simply performing a play without words is not only an injustice to the play and playwright, but a misrepresentation of pantomime as well.

Pantomime is, at its best, a delightful and engrossing medium of communication and expression, no matter if performed by amateur or professional. But the art is often misused. "Pantomime" in ballet and

14

opera tends, at some levels, toward the sterile and tedious. Even when performed competently, the pantomime may prove totally ineffective, due to context. Pantomime and modern dance, however, are more closely related, and share many principles in training and development which may be shared occasionally in performance, but again, not always effectively.

Pantomime can exist solely in the purist tradition and still hold some degree of relevance to "modern" theatre. Plays such as *Royal Hunt of the Sun* and *Rosencrantz and Guildenstern Are Dead,* for example, employ pantomime in context. The inclusion does not detract from the play, or from pantomime, but heightens the dramatic and artistic intent of both.

In any context, however, pantomime must be approached as pantomime, sufficient unto itself, not as "acting without words," as a "pantomime-dance," or a "skit." Isolationism has its limitations, but does avoid unnecessary conflicts in style, interpretation, and philosophy, in deference to the independence and integrity of the art and artist.

part two:

exercises

INTRODUCTION TO
THE EXERCISES

Part Two begins with exercises for the body, the face, and the hands and concludes with illusory exercises. Since the body is the only medium in pantomime through which a performer is able to communicate, it is vitally important that he know how to utilize and control even its subtlest movement. The main objectives in these exercises are the isolation and control of divisions and subdivisions of the body as well as a mental awareness of the physical sensations involved.

The exercises for the body progress in difficulty and should be attempted in the order described. The exercises for the face and hands are in no particular order as the difficulty is dependent upon the facility and dexterity of the individual.

EXERCISES FOR THE BODY

The exercises for the body consist of inclinations, rotations, and separations, each involving five divisions of the body: The head, the neck, the shoulders and

chest, the waist, and the hips (including the legs). All of these exercises are to be done standing erect and relaxed, heels together, feet at a ninety-degree angle to each other *(Figure 4)*. This position should be taken before and retained throughout each exercise, unless otherwise stated.

In the formative stages of development and study, it is helpful and advisable to use a full-length mirror so the movement and positions of the body can be discerned and, if necessary, corrected. As development progresses, it is best to do without the mirror, relying upon the instincts and training of the body in determining all movement and positions. In this way, a sense of "body-awareness" is assured correlative development.

INCLINATIONS

Inclinations are defined as the controlled bending of the body to the front, either side, or the back. Inclinations are the initial step toward isolation of controlling muscles of the body, and should be done slowly at first until a familiarity with the divisions of the body has de-

7

8

veloped, then with gradually increasing speed and flexibility. A smooth and controlled transition between the divisions of the body is of primary concern.

Front Inclination

Standing erect, relaxed. Heels together, feet at a ninety-degree angle to each other. Refer to *Figure 4* for the divisions of the body.

HEAD: The head falls forward as far as possible without bending the neck *(Figure 5)*.

NECK: The neck bends to allow the head to fall further forward, either to a position of resting on the chest or relatively close to that position *(Figure 6)*.

SHOULDERS AND

CHEST: The head and neck continue in the path of inclination into the chest. The chest should sink *(Figure 7)*. The feeling here is that the upper ribs are sliding down and behind the lower ribs.

WAIST: All sections of the body included so far now bend forward at the waist, retaining the same relative position *(Figure 8)*. To effect the waist inclination without involving the hips, it may

9

10

be necessary to tighten the hip muscles.

HIPS: With a relaxation of the hip muscles, the body will continue forward and down, with all sections of the body holding their relative positions *(Figure 9)*.

During the course of this exercise, the arms will hang relaxed at the side. The completion of this exercise is in the reversal of procedure, remembering that each section of the body must retain its relative position until relaxed from that position, in order.

Side Inclination

Standing erect, relaxed. Heels together, feet at a ninety-degree angle to each other.

The importance of the side inclination is that the body must remain on a flat plane, side to side, facing front at all times.

HEAD: The head falls to the side as far as possible without bending the neck *(Figure 10)*.

NECK: The neck bends to allow the head to fall further to the side *(Figure 11)*. The effect is to allow the ear to fall to the shoulder, without moving the shoulder. This is, of course, physically impossible for most people, but the effect should be the same.

SHOULDERS AND

CHEST: The head and neck continue in their path to the side. The shoulder opposite the path of inclination should rise as the shoulder in the direction of the inclination sinks *(Figure 12)*. Again the feeling of the upper ribs sliding down and behind the lower, on the side of inclination only.

WAIST: The upper body now bends at the waist in the direction of inclination. All positions of the body remain relative. The arm opposite the direction of inclination will fall across the body. The other will hang relaxed at the side *(Figure 13)*.

HIPS: To allow for the side inclination of the hips, it is necessary to bend the leg opposite the path of inclination. In other words, if the inclination is to the left, the right leg will bend *(Figure 14)*. The body will continue in a path to the side.

The completion of this exercise is in the reversal of procedure, and also in the inclination to the opposite side.

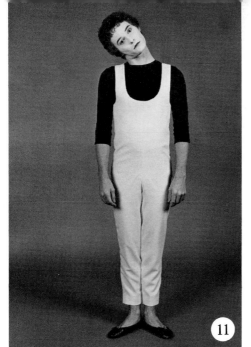

Back Inclination

For the back inclination the position of the feet is changed so that one foot is parallel and a medium stride ahead of the other. The weight of the body is centered *(Figure 15)*.

HEAD: The head is lifted as far as possible without bending the neck *(Figure 16)*. In most cases this will be a larger movement than expected.

NECK: The neck bends to allow the head to fall back, between the shoulder blades *(Figure 17)*. Eyes should be looking straight up, as a point of reference.

SHOULDERS AND

CHEST: Shoulders fall back as the chest is lifted up. The head falls further back *(Figure 18)*. The chest should be lifted straight up, rather than up and back.

WAIST: The body bends back at the waist as far as possible, still keeping balance. This will be a limited movement in most cases. The arms will fall back *(Figure 19)*.

HIPS: In order to include the hips in the back inclination, the back leg must be bent. The body will not move a great deal at this point *(Figu   )*. It may prove helpful if the knees are braced together when the back leg is bent. This should be discontinued as soon as possible.

The completion of this exercise is in the reversal of procedure, the changing of the extended leg, and the repetition of the entire exercise. The fully inclined position should not be held for any length of time until the muscles have developed sufficiently to withstand the strain.

Following the entire back inclination, a repetition of the front inclination may be helpful in relaxing, or to "even-up" the muscle strain.

ROTATIONS

Rotations are the controlled turning of the body, either to the left or right. The body rotates on an axis which extends from the top of the head, through the body, perpendicular to the floor. In doing a rotation, each section of the body rotates as far as possible without, and before, involving the next section. As with the inclinations, rotations should be done

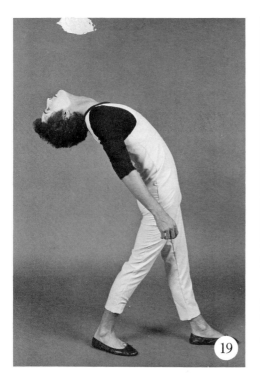

21

slowly at first, maintaining a smooth transition between divisions of the body.

Rotation

Standing erect, relaxed. Heels together, feet at a ninety-degree angle to each other *(Figure 4)*.

HEAD: The head rotates on the axis as far as possible without turning the neck *(Figure 21)*. This will be a rotation of about forty-five degrees from center.

NECK: The neck allows the head to turn to the side as far as possible, approximately ninety degrees from center *(Figure 22)*. At this point, the head should be straight, in a line perpendicular to the floor. A compensation, by tilting the head to either side, may be necessary.

SHOULDERS AND

CHEST: The shoulders and chest now rotate as a unit, head and neck follow, the rest of the body remaining forward, on center *(Figure 23)*. Again, be aware of the position of the head.

WAIST: The waist will not rotate to any great extent. It is simply a release of the waist muscles to allow the head, neck, and shoulders and chest to con-

tinue the rotation *(Figure 24)*.

HIPS: For the hip rotation it will be necessary, as in the Side Inclination, to bend the leg opposite the path of rotation. The leg should also rotate, to a limited extent, on the ball of the foot, in the direction of rotation *(Figure 25)*. Avoid the tendency to incline forward in the direction of rotation. The body must remain upright and perpendicular to the floor.

The completion of this exercise is in the reversal of procedure and in the rotation to the opposite side.

SEPARATIONS

The isolation and control of the divisional muscles of the body are most apparent in the Separations. They involve, in effect, the separation of parts of the body from other parts, or divisions, of the body—movement that is unrelated to any natural bodily function, such as bending or turning. Consequently, separations are the most difficult single concept of movement to master, and should be attempted only after a firm foundation in muscular con-

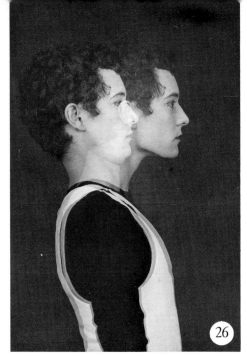

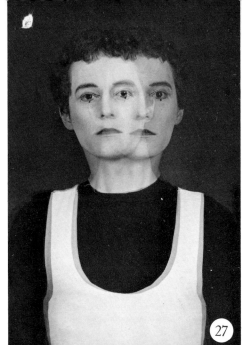

trol, through inclinations and rotations, has been established.

Separations

As a preparatory exercise to the separation of the entire body, the isolated separation of the head and neck will facilitate understanding of the type of movement involved.

It is imperative that the first attempts at separations be done in front of a mirror. Only then can a correlation between movement and sensation be maintained.

Separation of the Head and Neck

1. The head is thrust forward and back, as far as possible, as if the chin were resting on a flat plane, parallel to the floor *(Figure 26)*.
2. The head is now moved from side to side, again as if the chin were on a flat plane. The face remains forward *(Figure 27)*.
3. Starting from a center position, the head is now rotated in either direction by, first, a forward separation, followed by a circular movement to either a left or right separation, then to a back separation, and continuing around the opposite side to a for-

ward separation once again *(Figure 28)*.

Separation—Divisions of the Body

Standing erect, relaxed. Heels together, feet at a ninety-degree angle to each other. All movement in this separation will be at the same time parallel and perpendicular to the floor. Refer to the photographs for movement and relative positions of the body.

HEAD: The head moves to the side, parallel and perpendicular to the floor, approximately half the distance that the head and neck can move together *(Figure 29)*.

NECK: The neck allows the head to move to the side as far as possible, still parallel and perpendicular to the floor *(Figure 30)*.

SHOULDERS AND

CHEST: The shoulders and chest, as a unit, slide to the side. This is a very subtle movement. The shoulders should be parallel to the floor. It may be necessary to compensate by raising or lowering either shoulder. At this point in the exercise, the arms will begin moving to the side, in the direction of

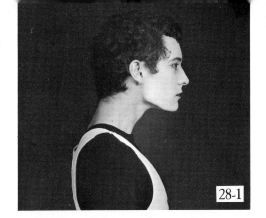

28-2

28-1

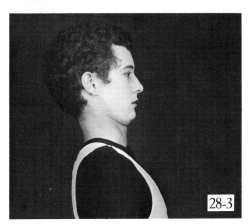

28-4

28-3

27

separation. The arm in the path of inclination will lead by the elbow, the opposite arm by the wrist. Hands remain relaxed, elbows bent *(Figure 31)*.

WAIST: The waist allows a continuation of the movement to the side of all sections included thus far. This will be a larger movement than those previous. Arms continue to the side *(Figure 32)*.

HIPS: To include the hip separation, the leg opposite the path of inclination bends, allowing the movement to be complete to the side *(Figure 33)*.

The completion of this exercise is in the reversal of procedure and in the separation to the opposite side. The fully separated position should not be held for any length of time until the muscles have developed sufficiently to withstand the effort.

VARIATIONS AND COMBINATIONS

Once the basic exercises have been established, many variations and combi-

31

32

nations are possible, utilizing the principles of each exercise related either to itself or to another. Included in this chapter are those exercises which are most relevant to the development of awareness and expansion of the means of physical expression. Only after the inclinations, rotations, and separations have been fixed in mind and body should these variations and combinations be attempted.

Variations

The previous exercises have followed a definite progression of movement and a retrogression, or reverse order, of the same movement. In this variation, however, half an exercise is done in the prescribed order, followed by the same order of movement done in the opposite direction. For example:

Variation of the Front Inclination

The exercise progresses in the proper order until the fully inclined position has been attained. The exercise then proceeds as follows:

HEAD: The head returns as far as possible to its original position, without returning the neck (*Figure 34*).

33

NECK: The neck returns to its original position, relative to the body at this point. The head will also have returned to its original, relative position *(Figure 35)*.

SHOULDERS AND

CHEST: The shoulders and chest return to their original, relative position *(Figure 36)*. At this point, the upper body should be relatively parallel to the floor.

WAIST: The waist returns to its original, relative position *(Figure 37)*.

HIPS: The body now returns, in its entirety, to its original position *(Figure 38)*.

This same procedure can be applied to the side and back inclinations. These will be more difficult due to balance and strain problems which will become evident as the exercise progresses.

Rotation Variation

The same procedure described in the inclination variation can be applied to the rotation—each section of the body returns to its original, relative position until the entire body has returned to the original position of the exercise.

35

36

37

38

 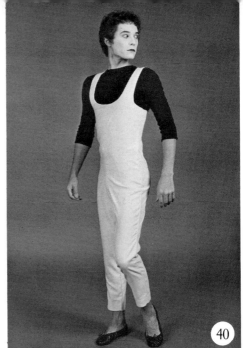

Another variation progresses as follows:

The fully rotated position is achieved. Then:

HEAD AND NECK: The head and neck not only return to their original, relative positions, but continue in a rotation to the opposite side *(Figure 39)*.

SHOULDERS AND

CHEST: Shoulders and chest follow head and neck into a rotation to the opposite side *(Figure 40)*.

WAIST: The waist allows a continuation of the rotation *(Figure 41)*.

HIPS: As the hips rotate, the leg that was bent will straighten as the opposite leg bends, allowing the rotation to reach its culmination at the opposite side *(Figure 42)*.

Since the movement flows through the original position of the exercise, the completion of this variation is the usual procedure for the completion of the basic rotation.

Separation Variation

The same procedure described in the inclination and rotation variations can also

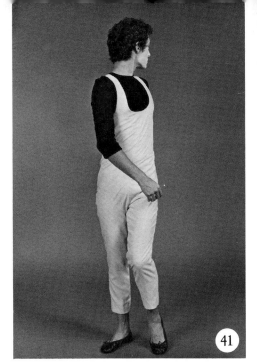

be applied to the separation. The separation variations will be much more difficult than any preceding variations, however, and should be done with the aid of a mirror.

Figures 43 to 46 illustrate the variation which returns to the central, original position.

Figures 47 to 50 illustrate the variation which flows through the central position to a separation to the opposite side.

Note that in both variations the head and neck function as a unit.

Combinations

All of the exercises thus far, including the variations, are based on single concepts of movement—bending, turning, or separating. The following are combinations of these single concepts to effect further exploration of physical awareness and development.

Combination Rotation and Front Inclination

HEAD: The head rotates, either left or right, as in the basic rotation, then inclines forward, in the direction of rotation (*Figure 51*).

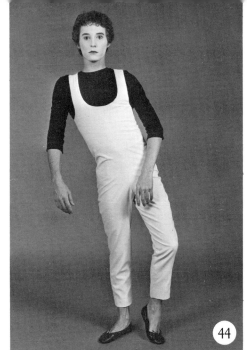

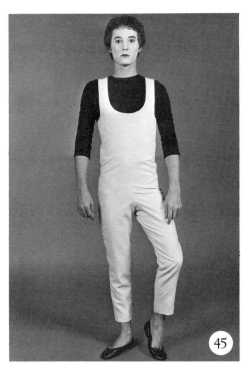

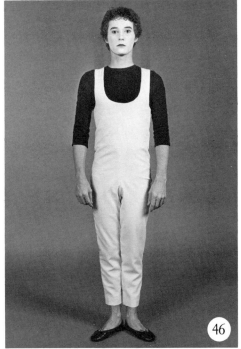

47

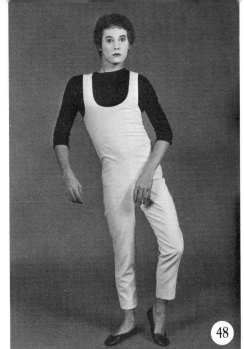

48

49

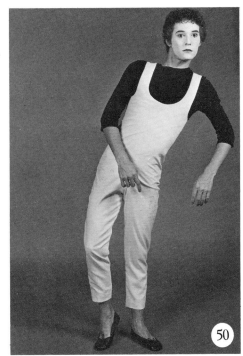

50

51

NECK: The neck allows the head to continue the rotation and inclination *(Figure 52)*.

SHOULDERS AND

CHEST: The shoulders and chest now rotate, then incline *(Figure 53)*. All sections of the body included so far should retain their relative positions. The arms should now be involved in the exercise.

WAIST: The waist allows continuation of the rotation-inclination *(Figure 54)*.

HIPS: The rotation progresses as far as possible. The leg opposite the direction of rotation will bend. The inclination is then completed, resulting in a position somewhat related to the "discus thrower" *(Figure 55)*.

The completion of this exercise is in the reversal of procedure—return of the inclination followed by a return of the rotation, a section at a time—and in repetition of the entire exercise to the opposite side.

Combination Separation and Front Inclination

HEAD: The head first separates, then in-

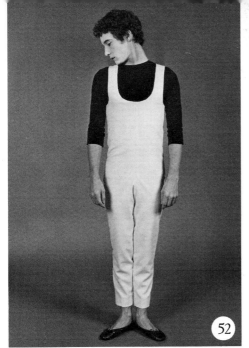

52

53

54

55

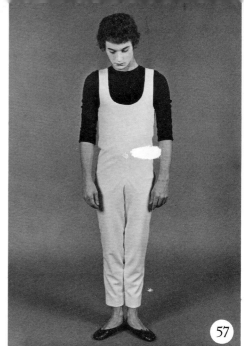

clines forward *(Figure 56)*.

The exercise continues in the same manner through the divisions of the body *(Figures 57 to 60)*. The completion of the exercise is, again, a reversal of procedure and a repetition to the opposite side.

Other combinations and variations are, for the most part, impractical or impossible, due primarily to a balancing problem, but may be attempted to the satisfaction of the individual.

EXERCISES FOR THE FACE AND HANDS

EXERCISES FOR THE FACE

Facial expression is an essential element in the performance of pantomime. The importance of the face is often minimized in deference to an increased emphasis upon the expressive competence of the body in total physical communication, regardless of the influence of facial expression. But without the animating qualities of the face, movement becomes contrived, characterization sterile and tedious, and an art is relegated to the level of an ineffectual

exercise. To modify a familiar thesis, the expression of the whole is equal only to the sum of *all* its parts.

The exercises for the face consist of five basic facial expressions—happy, sad, surprised, angry, and fearful—each involving a particular set or combination of facial muscles. This is by no means the complete list of expressions, but those from which others are derived. The variations are endless, depending on the facility and imagination of the individual. All of the following are, for the purpose of an exercise, exaggerations or approximations of any true expression, but are entirely acceptable for performance when used in the proper context. The main objective in these exercises is the development of increased flexibility and control of the face in addition to a greater range of facial expression.

The five basic expressions:

These expressions vary considerably from person to person. In attempting to duplicate the expressions in the photographs, each individual should find his own facial approximation of the desired expression.

38

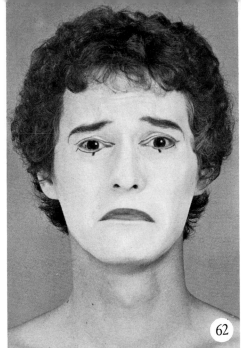

HAPPY: All the muscles of the face are up-lifted in an expression of unequivocal joy. Eyebrows are raised, as well as cheek muscles. The eyes will squint, more or less, depending on the individual. The mouth forms a large, open smile *(Figure 61)*.

SAD: Facial muscles are pulled down. Inner corners of the eyebrows are pulled up. Mouth forms a frown *(Figure 62)*.

SURPRISED: The face is drawn up and down. Eyebrows are raised. The mouth forms an exaggerated "oh" *(Figure 63)*.

ANGRY: Of all the expressions, anger is the most difficult to duplicate or form even an acceptable approximation. For the purpose of this exercise, the expression of anger entails the drawing or bunch-ing of the muscles towards the nose. The nose wrinkles, eyes squint, eye-brows furrow, and the mouth forms somewhat of a frown, almost a pucker *(Figure 64)*. Individual facial differ-ences will be most apparent in this expression.

FEARFUL: The face forms a variation of the upper half of "sad" and the lower

half of "happy." Eyes open as wide as possible *(Figure 65)*.

Starting with "happy," progress slowly through all the expressions, letting one expression overlap the next. Repeat in re-verse order.

In any order, progress rapidly through the expressions, returning to a normal, relatively expressionless face between each.

In any order, progress both rapidly and slowly through the expressions, some-times overlapping, sometimes not, at will.

EXERCISES FOR THE HANDS

The exercises for the hands are de-signed to facilitate digital and subdigital isolation and control. Inasmuch as the hands are the primary tool of delineation, expansion of the means of this form of expression can only enhance the overall effectiveness of a performance. These exer-cises must be done slowly. The develop-ment of the muscles will take a good deal of time and effort, and any attempt to accelerate the process will prove un-successful. The following serve not only to develop isolation and control, but also

63

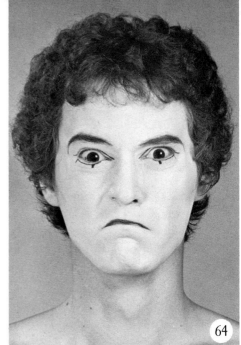

64

will strengthen the hands and fingers considerably.

Digital Isolation and Control

1. Rotate each finger independently in its socket, clockwise and counterclockwise, then move each finger linearly—up and down, and side to side. Fingers remain straight. Sympathetic movement between fingers should kept to a minimum.

2. Fingers together, move outer fingers away from inner fingers and return, hands separately and together.

3. Fingers slightly spread, move inner fingers to outer fingers and return, hands separately and together.

4. Hands out, palms up. First, hands separately. Starting with the little finger of either hand, close the hand by rolling in each finger, one at a time. Open the hand in reverse order, that is, starting with the index finger. Repeat with other hand, then hands together. Repeat entire exercise beginning with the index finger of either hand.

5. Starting with the little finger of either hand, repeat closing procedure, then

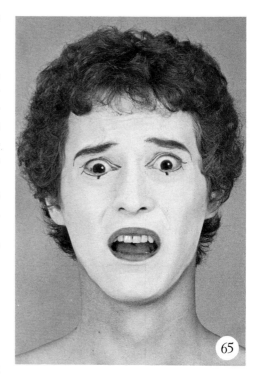

65

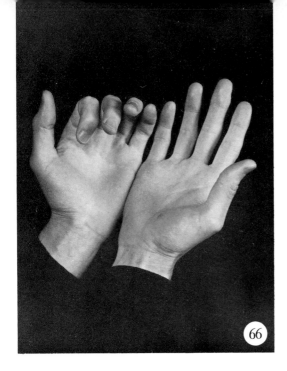

66

open the hand, starting with the same little finger. Repeat with other hand, then together. Repeat entire exercise, starting with the index finger, either hand.

Repeat exercises 4 and 5.

6. Hands out, palms up, hands slightly touching. Starting with the index finger of the left hand, roll the fingers closed, in order, to the index finger of the right hand until both hands are closed *(Figure 66)*. Open the hands in reverse order; that is, starting with the index finger of the right hand, roll the fingers open, in order, to the index finger of the left hand.

Starting with the index finger of the right hand, repeat the exercise.

7. Starting with the index finger of the left hand, repeat the closing procedure. Open the fingers, in order, starting with the same index finger. Repeat, starting with the index finger of the right hand.

Repeat exercises 6 and 7.

8. Hands out, left palm down, right palm up, hands slightly touching. Starting with the little finger of the

left hand, roll the fingers closed, in order, to the index finger of the right hand. Open in reverse order. Repeat closing, then open, starting with the same little finger of the left hand. Repeat the exercise, starting with the index finger, right hand. Repeat the entire exercise, left palm up, right palm down.

Subdigital Isolation and Control

1. Isolate controlling muscles of the middle knuckle of each finger, both hands *(Figure 67)*. First, each finger separately, then in combination.

2. Isolate controlling muscles of the top knuckle of each finger, separately, and in combination *(Figure 68)*.

To effect the preceding isolations, hold firmly that part of the finger that should *not* move, allowing only the isolated knuckle to function. This should provide an acquaintance with the sensation of the isolation. Repeat as often as necessary until the isolation is attained, without support.

3. Fingers straight. Bend middle knuckle *(Figure 69)*, then top knuckle *(Figure 70)*, of each finger, separately

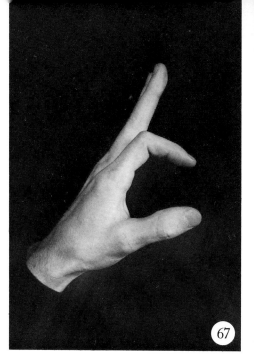

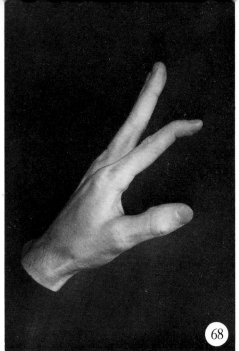

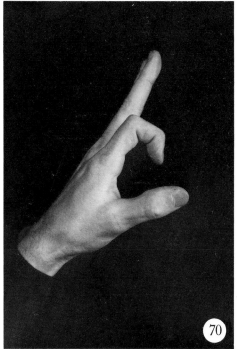

43

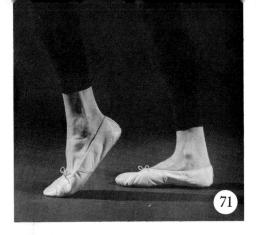

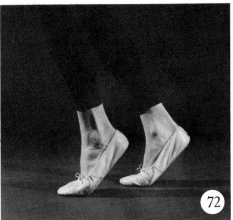

and in combination.

Subdigital isolation is an inherent trait in some individuals and need only be reinforced. The isolation of the top knuckle serves a very limited purpose in pantomime, but should be realized for increased physical awareness and possible application in performance.

ILLUSORY EXERCISES

The illusory exercises are included here for the first time in any published form. Covered are most of the illusions of locomotion encountered in pantomime. The illusory effect of each is that of moving from place to place, without actually going anywhere. These exercises range from easy to difficult, and demand a great deal of time and effort. The timing, balance, and coordination of even the simplest exercise cannot be mastered in a single day, and should not be used in performance for months.

In approaching these exercises, establish a firm method of study. Attempt one pattern or division of movement at a time. Develop it thoroughly. Then the second

74

pattern. Combine the two. Move on to the third pattern. Combine one, two, and three, and so on. Allow ample time for development and awareness of every movement pattern. Following the completion of each exercise, do it backwards (except Skating), and in slow motion. Remember that the transfer of weight must also be in slow motion, in addition to the movement patterns. Remain constantly aware. A mistake, a hesitation, or an inaccuracy in movement will completely destroy an illusion.

The illusory exercises are stylized. In other words, the illusions are not exactly or entirely correct, but have been adapted to performance to appear correct. "Stylized" is not to be confused with "style," the "distinguishable individuality" of a performer. The format of each exercise is standard. Individuality makes them different.

STAIRS

Feet and legs: Raise either foot in a small arc, taking a small step forward (approximately 6 inches), pointing toe,

coming to rest on the ball of the foot *(Figure 71)*. Raise up in the balls of both feet *(Figure 72)*. Down on the flat of the first foot *(Figure 73)*. Second foot will be in a position to repeat sequence. Repeat, one foot at a time, then alternate. Take a slight pause between each sequence. There will be a slight forward movement, depending on the size of the step taken.

Arms and hands: Usually, only one arm is used to denote a railing. Ascending: The hand grasps the rail approximately eye-level, and as each step is taken, progresses in a diagonal path downward, to slightly behind the level of the body. *(Figure 74 shows body position, ascending.)* The arm moves only as the performer rises on the balls of both feet. The length of time it takes to complete the arm movement is based on the rate of climb, size of stairs, condition of the character, and other factors. Experiment individually. Descending: The foot sequence remains the same. By changing the position and direction of movement of the rail hand, descending stairs is defined. Grasp the rail, arm extended, as far as possible in a downward diagonal. Progress through the foot se-

quence, moving the arm diagonally upward to chest level.

In either direction, the rail may be grasped again in the pause between the alternating foot sequence. Also, the head and eyes focus in the direction of the supposed movement, up or down.

The final step in ascending or descending may be designated by definitely placing the foot flat on the floor, in place of the next imaginary stair, then naturally walking away from the stairs, dropping the rail arm to the side or definitely removing it from the rail. This is not mandatory for the final step. Simply moving away from the stairs, or changing direction in movement will usually signal the end of the stairs. In any possibly confusing context, definitely end the stairs.

This illusion is only effective when viewed from the side, or from a slight angle. There is no illusion when viewed directly from the front.

FRONT ILLUSORY WALK

Feet and legs: Begin by spreading legs comfortably apart, to the side, feet parallel.

Rock side to side until the heel opposite the direction of motion rises off the floor. Keep the upper body relatively stiff. Continue. As the heel of either foot comes off the floor, point the toe, then raise the entire foot off the floor. As the body motion returns, replace the foot in a toe-heel manner, with a definite placement of both the toe and the heel. (The toe is actually the ball of the foot.) Knees should flex with the movement. As the foot is replaced, it should touch the floor in somewhat of a "toe-in" so that the feet remain parallel.

Now establish a definite rhythm to the motion. As the body reaches either the left or right limit of motion, execute a separation of the waist, shoulders and chest, head and neck, as a unit, to the opposite side, and continue the motion. The separation should occur as the heel of the foot touches the floor. Shortly thereafter, the leg should straighten, moving the body in the opposite direction.

Arms are slightly bent, one hand pointing to the opposite knee, crossing the body, the other moves beside and slightly behind the level of the body. *Figures 75 and 76* show the limit of movement to

either side before the separation, and the position of the body at that time. *Figure 77* shows the relative position of the limits of motion to the middle, neutral position, as well as the relative movement of the head through the air. The head progresses in a flattened-out figure eight pattern. As the body reaches the limit of movement to either side, the straightening of the leg raises the level of the head, down through the middle position, to the opposite side.

The illusion is effective only from the front, or at a slight angle.

SIDE ILLUSORY WALK

Feet and legs: Lift foot, pointing toe *(Figure 78)*. Move foot in a small arc forward, extending heel, straighten leg, slightly flex toes backwards *(Figure 79)*. Begin to bring foot back to its original position. At the same time, flex the knee of the opposite leg, rise to the ball of the foot before the first foot returns to its original position. The first foot will not have touched the floor as yet *(Figure 80)*. (This "flip" is the most important part of the walk.) Slide the first foot along the floor

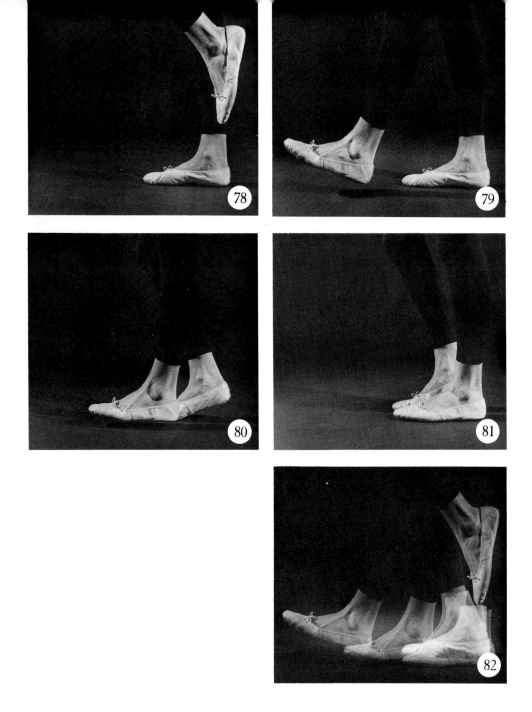

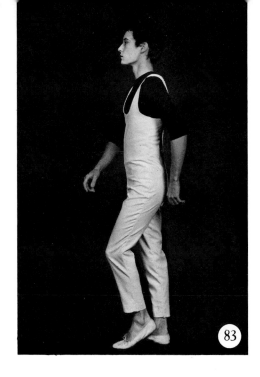

83

to its original position *(Figure 81)*. The second foot is now in position to begin the sequence. Repeat the entire sequence, feet separately, then alternately. At the point in the movement when the first foot returns to its original position, begin the sequence with the other foot, maintaining a smooth transition. *Figure 82* shows the relative position of the foot in each section of the sequence. There should be little, if any, forward movement. If movement is desired, replace the foot either ahead or behind its original position.

The next part of the exercise is called "taking in the slack." Since the head must remain level, not bob up and down, the rise and fall of the feet is taken up somewhere between the feet and the head. This may be accomplished by a slight flex in the knees, the pelvis (usually), or waist (for females, a slight side to side movement, from the waist down—a natural function in most cases).

Arms and hands: The hand, led by the wrist, points to the opposite knee, slightly crossing the body. The other arm moves to the side and slightly behind the level of the body *(Figure 83)*. Both arms

are slightly bent at all times. The movement of the arms will seem awkward and unnatural at first. The tendency is for simultaneous rather than opposing movement between arms and legs.

This illusion is most effective when viewed from the side, or at very slight angles. It may be viewed from the front if the arm movement is exaggerated. This will not be totally effective, however. The front illusory walk would better suit the purpose.

BICYCLE

The basic position for the bicycle is shown in *Figure 84* (less affectations).

Feet and legs: The feet move in a pattern similar to the side illusory walk. Only the foot closest to the audience is used. The pattern is modified to allow the foot to move in a complete circle, not simply in a forward arc. The "flip" remains, occurring as the first foot passes through its original position. The performer actually balances on one foot, except when moving from place to place, because the first foot should not rest on

the ground at any time during its circular motion. The sequence is repeated rapidly for the effect *(Figure 85)*.

Changing the position of the body and moving from place to place is accomplished by taking quick, tiny steps, in the rhythm of the bicycle, returning to the bicycle sequence as soon as possible.

A "one-foot hop-turn" is sometimes used for going around corners or changing direction. One foot is extended diagonally to the side as the performer hops on the other foot, retaining the basic bicycle position *(Figure 86)*. (Think of a silent movie chase, on foot, around a corner.)

The bicycle illusion is effective only when viewed from the side.

SKATING

Skating is a difficult illusion to perform convincingly, because the feet are unaccustomed to moving in the manner described. There is also a danger of sprained ankles in this exercise. The progression should therefore be slow and careful, allowing for complete development of all muscles involved. A smooth, clean floor, not overly slippery, is essential to this exercise.

Feet and legs: (1) Standing on one foot, move from side to side by alternating heel-toe, heel-toe across the floor. Alternate feet so that the movement is both to the left and to the right. (2) Establish a definite rhythm to the movement, slow at first, then slightly faster with each repetition. Knees should flex. (3) Do three repetitions of "heel-toe" to each side. Pause on the last "toe" in each direction, then push off in the opposite direction, keeping knees flexed. Assembling all the pieces of this puzzle, the rhythm is as follows: Counting one through eight, numbers one through five consist of heel-toe-heel-toe-heel; number six, the final "toe" simply comes to rest on the floor, rather than taking another step to the side; seven and eight, rest on the flat of the foot, prepare to move to the opposite side.

Figure 87 shows the limit of movement to the left. Note that the foot off the floor is preparing to move to the right. *Figure 88* shows the action just before the limit of movement to the right. The arms are still moving up and away from the body, even though the body has ceased perceptible movement.

The entire exercise may cover from three to six feet, or more, of floor space, depending on speed of movement, size of steps, size of feet, enthusiasm, and energy exerted. By bending forward at the waist and moving from side to side at a faster rate, the skater will also appear to move faster. By standing more erect and moving a little slower, the skater will adopt a more leisurely attitude. The feet must move fast enough, however, that the illusion is of gliding, not plodding, across the floor (imaginary ice).

The illusion is most effective when viewed from the front. The effect diminishes as the angle from the audience increases.

CLOSING NOTES
PART TWO

Often a potentially good, imaginative, or stimulating performance is marred by the performer's inability to use his body expressively. Either he is unaware of what his body is doing, or he is unable to control his movement in accordance with his wishes. His creativity is stifled by his lack of physical discipline. The point is, com-munication of any performer's ideas is entirely dependent upon the performer's own technical physical ability. For any movement to be expressive, the performer must understand, be aware of, what he is doing. However his body functions, he must understand it, exactly as it is. The discipline of awareness is difficult to attain, but invaluable and indispensable.

It may be argued that strict discipline, of either a mental or physical nature, inhibits spontaneity. While it is true that pantomime is a highly developed, technical discipline, it should be understood that the discipline is instrumental but secondary, and that a meaningful, expressive performance must occur spontaneously. By spontaneity, however, I do not mean "chance-happening" or "impulsive-coincidental occurrence," but rather the unmistakable quality of sincerity apparent in expression. The expression must seem uncontrived and natural, although it may have been rehearsed endless times. The essential element of "naturalness" is the sincerity of the mind which does not deviate from its chosen objective, or the means to that objective. The concept of artistry is, at the same time, discipline in spontaneity, and spontaneity in discipline.

52

part three:

mime and pantomime

MIME AND PANTOMIME

The words "mime" and "pantomime" (meaning the art) are often used alternatively, yet they are not synonymous, at least as far as I am concerned. In simplest terms, a pantomime is an illustration of a story. It depends heavily upon accurately described objects, actions, situations, and events to tell this story. Mime, on the other hand, may tell a story, but regards the conventions of experience and of the stage as too explicit, and relies upon a more implicit, more abstract approach to the theme, which is of greater importance in mime than the means of presentation. Pantomime is explicit, whereas mime is ambiguous. But to be ambiguous is not necessarily detrimental. In mime there is no right or wrong interpretation. When I write or perform a mime, I form my own opinions, my own interpretation for the piece. This does not, however, preclude any interpretation that a member of an audience may form while observing the same piece. Each performer and observer develops his own interpretations, associations, and symbolic references, using his own imagination, relating to what is taking place on stage. In this way, each concept, based on any frame of reference, is valid, no matter how simple or elaborate it may be. The essence of mime is in the diversity of interpretations, and in the great amount of "responsive imagination," in the area of interpretation, that may result from its performance.

There is less questioning of motivations and situations in pantomime than in mime. A mime is dependent upon questions, not only in the area of interpretation, but also, perhaps, in the area of presentation. A good mime, like a good pantomime, must progress smoothly and rapidly, but not necessarily simply or clearly, since the premise itself is in question, clarity and simplicity being secondary to the effect.

Another distinction between mime and pantomime, only indirectly related to "responsive imagination," is subject matter. A pantomime can cover any subject, from an ant to the universe, with reasonably equal success. Mime takes this basic concept one step further. It deals not only with the physical aspects of the ant and the universe, but also with any underlying

54

motivation, question, or implication in its existence, function, or merit. Mime also presents situations that otherwise could not or might not exist, for the express purpose of posing questions, or offering a perusal and perspective of that which could or might happen, given a number of alternative situations which are limited only by imagination. Pantomime deals with the physical world. Mime deals with the physical world, its implications, and its interpretations—a much broader, and less conclusive range of subject matter.

All mime relies, to some extent, upon the elements of pantomime, and in this way exists not as a subdivision, but as a coexistent of the art of silence. The communication between individuals, expressed only through the movement and gestures of the body, remains the essence of the art. The objective is constant. The difference lies only in the approach.

NOTES ON PERFORMANCE

The following mimes are intended as examples of symbolic reference, in gesture and movement, to various thoughts, ideas,

and feelings—all my own. I do not intend to elaborate upon the symbolism further. To do so, I would run the risk of my comments being misconstrued as the basis for interpretive judgment. This could only prove detrimental, and should have no bearing whatsoever on any performance. I would, however, like to comment on the physical performance of these mimes, based upon my own experience with them.

First of all, the written word is only an approximation of any actual movement. In most cases it is an oversimplification. Even so, the directions for movement should be followed as closely as possible. Secondly, the movement in each mime should progress smoothly and relatively quickly; there should be no stopping between movements except in the case of a written "pause." Each pause should amount to no more than two or three seconds, or counts. Once a mime is begun, movement should continue at relatively the same tempo, or speed. Subtle changes in tempo are necessary to avoid a monotonous flow of movement; however, abrupt changes in tempo will result in an ineffective performance. Finally, facial expression should be limited to those written, whenever possible. Some natural facial reactions will occur and need not be eliminated unless inappropriate to the theme or mood set by the performance.

The approach of these mimes must be simple and direct. The first two, "Mime for Three Players" and "The Pawn, the Bishop, and the King" are serious attempts at symbolic reference. (The props cited in "The Pawn, the Bishop, and the King" are included only for a better communication of the theme to the audience. The intention should be to stimulate the imagination of the audience, not confuse it. Props are added as a concession to this intention.) "Exercise in Five Acts" and "The Human Race" are lighter, more "tongue-in-cheek" in nature, but still retain a basic, underlying motivation. The theme is of primary importance in any mime. A simple, straightforward performance will enhance its impression.

Mime
for
Three
Players

in three parts

The setting consists of three large blocks, of equal size, set and spaced as in the diagram at the beginning of each part.

One: Lights

Lights up full.

Two men are discovered sitting, facing front (toward the audience), one on each of the two downstage blocks. A woman is sitting, facing front, on the block upstage and between them.

As the lights come up, the left stage man cowers. He looks for a place out of the light. He rises. Crosses to behind his own block. Sits on the floor, his back to his block.

As this is taking place, the right stage man sits more erect. He straightens his clothes. Sits looking toward the light.

Pause.

The lights now begin to fade.

The right stage man starts to slump over slightly. He rises. Crosses to behind his block. Sits on the floor, his back to his block. (The lights should now be at a level which permits observance of the players, but no more than ½ full.)

Pause.

The left stage man rises. Crosses to the front of his block. Sits on the block. Sits more erect. Straightens his clothes. Sits looking into the darkness.

Pause.

The lights now come up full.

Left stage man again cowers. Looks for a place out of the light. Crosses to behind his block. Sits on the floor, his back to his block.

Pause.

Right stage man rises. Crosses to the front of his block. Sits on block. Sits more erect. Straightens his clothes. Sits looking into the light.

Pause.

The lights now fade in the left stage area,

but remain up full right stage.

The right stage man remains sitting erect, looking into the light. The left stage man rises. Crosses to the front of his block. Sits on his block. Sits more erect. Straightens his clothes. Sits looking into the darkness.

Pause.

The woman now rises. Crosses to behind her block. Sits on the floor, her back to her block.

The lights now fade to ½ on right stage. Lights up full left stage.

Both men begin to slump as the lights change. They both rise (not necessarily in unison). Cross to behind their respective blocks. Sit on the floor, with their backs to their blocks.

Pause.

The lights now fade to ½ left stage. The entire stage is now ½ full.

Pause.

The lights now come up full on both sides of the stage. The entire stage is now fully illuminated.

Pause.

The lights fade out completely.

End of part *one*.

Two: Binoculars   □□□

Lights up full.

Woman discovered sitting on center block, facing front, holding binoculars.

Pause.

She rises. Puts binoculars to her eyes. Looks left. Looks right. Looks front. Takes binoculars from her eyes. Sits on block.

Pause.

First man enters from left, binoculars to his eyes. He crosses to center stage, directly in front of the woman. He faces front. Looks left. Looks right. Faces right. Exits right.

Pause.

Same man enters from right, walking backwards, binoculars to his eyes. Turns front. Crosses to center stage. Faces front. Looks right. Looks left. Faces left. Takes one step left, in front of left stage block. Faces front. Takes binoculars from his

58

eyes. Sits on left stage block.

Pause.

They kiss. They hold the kiss throughout the following:

Pause.

Second man enters from right, binoculars to his eyes. (The binoculars are held backwards by the second man.) He crosses to center stage directly in front of the woman. He faces front. Looks right. Looks left. Faces left. Exits left.

Pause.

Second man enters from left, walking backwards, binoculars to his eyes (still backwards). He turns front. Crosses to center. Faces front. Looks left. Looks right. Faces right. Takes one step right, in front of right stage block. Faces front. Takes binoculars from his eyes. Sits on the right stage block.

As he sits, the kiss is terminated.

Pause.

The woman and the second man now kiss. They hold the kiss throughout the following:

Pause.

First man now rises. Turns his binoculars backwards. Puts binoculars to his eyes. Looks right. Looks left. Faces left. Exits left.

Pause.

The kiss is terminated.

Second man rises. Turns his binoculars frontwards. Puts binoculars to his eyes. Looks left. Looks right. Faces right. Exits right.

Pause.

The woman now rises. Puts binoculars to her eyes. Looks left. Looks right. Looks front. Takes binoculars from her eyes. Sits on block.

Pause.

Lights fade out completely.

End of part *two*.

Note: The binoculars are held in both hands at all times. There is no actual physical contact between players at any time. The kiss is approximated without lips touching.

Three: Fallen man

Lights up full.

Two men are discovered, one on each downstage block, sitting back to back, somewhat slumped over, sleeping. A woman stands upstage and between them, in front of the upstage block.

Pause.

The woman prods the first man, right stage. He does not move. She prods again. He awakens. Looks front. Rises. Crosses to left of second man, left stage. First man stands facing second man. First man looks front. Looks to second man.

Pause.

First man strikes second man who promptly falls off his block. First man returns to his own block. Sits. Looks front. Turns right. Slumps over, falling asleep.

Second man rises from the floor. Straightens his clothes. Looks left. Looks front. Returns to his block. Sits on his block. Looks front. Turns left. Slumps over, falling asleep.

Pause.

The woman prods second man, left stage. He does not move. She prods again. He awakens. Looks front. Turns left. Slumps over, falling asleep.

Pause.

Woman prods first man. He awakens. Looks front. Rises. Crosses to left of second man. Stands facing second man. Looks front. Looks to second man.

Pause.

First man strikes second man who again falls off his block. First man returns to his block. Sits on his block. Looks front. Turns right. Slumps over, falling asleep.

Second man rises from the floor. Straightens his clothes. Looks right. Looks front. Returns to his block. Sits on his block. Looks front. Turns left. Slumps over, falling asleep.

Pause.

Woman prods second man. He awakens. Looks front. Turns left. Slumps over, falling asleep.

Pause.

Woman prods first man. He awakens.

60

Looks front. Rises. Crosses to left of second man. Stands facing second man. Looks front. Looks to second man.

Second man suddenly falls off his block.

First man looks to second man. Looks front. Looks to woman. Looks front. Returns to his block while looking at second man. First man sits on his block. Looks front.

Woman sits on her block.

Second man rises. Straightens his clothes. Looks to first man.

First man rises. Crosses to right of woman. Stands facing the woman. Looks front. Looks to woman.

Pause. Pause.

First man strikes the woman who promptly falls off her block, at the feet of the second man.

Second man looks to woman.

First man looks front. Crosses to the right of his block. Sits on his block.

Second man looks to first man as first man looks front. First man turns right. Slumps over, falling asleep.

Second man looks front. Assumes a puzzled expression.

Lights fade out completely.

End of part *three*. End of "Mime for Three Players."

The Pawn
the Bishop
and the King

Bare stage.

A blue light fades in on right stage area.

First player (male) is discovered standing right center, facing upstage, holding a stick which symbolizes a rifle.

Second player (male or female) is discovered standing up center left, facing downstage.

Pause.

Second player looks off right. Looks front. Crosses to first player. Turns first player to face downstage. Second player returns up left center. Looks off right. Looks front.

Pause.

First player looks off right. Salutes with his left hand, holds stick in his right. Holding salute, he looks front. Looks off right. Holding salute, looking off right, he puts stick on floor. Stands erect. Mimes waving a small flag over his head with his right hand. Looks front, saluting and waving. Looks off right. Drops his right hand to his side. Picks up the stick. Stands erect. Looks front. Looks off right. Drops his left hand to his side. Looks front.

Pause.

First player looks off right. Puts stick to his left shoulder. Looks front. Looks off right. Looks front. Executes a left face. Looks off right, over his shoulder. Begins marching in place. As he is marching, he looks directly in front of himself (off left). Looks off right, over his shoulder. Halts. Executes a right face, still looking off right. Looks front.

Pause.

First player looks off right. Takes stick from his shoulder to a position of "ready." Hunches over as if to advance upon an enemy. Looks front. Looks off right. Looks front. Makes a fierce, determined expression, as if a mask. Looks off right. Begins advancing in place. Looks front. Looks off right. Looks front. Fires his stick rifle towards left center. Looks off right. Turns and fires his stick rifle down right. Looks off right. Faces front as if to fire again. He is shot. He stops advancing. Slowly his face falls, taking on a pained, puzzled, unbelieving expression. He clutches his stomach with his left hand, holding the stick rifle in his right.

He looks off right. Looks front. Attempts to look up, but is dissuaded and looks off right. Still clutching his stomach, he puts down his stick. Stands not quite erect. Salutes with his right hand. Looks front. Looks off right. Mimes waving a small flag with his right hand. Looks front. Attempts to look up, but is again dissuaded. Looks off right. Stops waving flag. Drops his right hand to his side. Looks front. Looks off right. Again salutes. Looks front. Looks off right. Holding salute, he slowly crumples to the floor, still looking off right. (The saluting hand is the last part of the body to fall to the floor. It should fall away from the body, palm up.)

Pause.

Second player looks off right. Looks front. Crosses to first player. Helps first player to his feet. Hands him his stick. Turns him to face upstage. Second player stands facing downstage.

Second player looks off right. Looks front. Exits off left. Re-enters, walking backwards, leading on third player (male) who holds a cross slightly aloft in his right hand. Second player leads third player to left center, slightly upstage of the level of the first player. Second player faces front.

Second player looks off right. Crosses to first player. Stands left of first player, facing front.

Pause.

Third player now assumes an ecclesiastical pose by (1) extending his left arm to the side, (2) then forearm and hand to a ninety-degree angle, (3) folding over the last two fingers under the thumb, and (4) extending the first two fingers together.

Pause.

Second player looks off right. Looks front. Turns first player to face downstage. Second player faces front. Looks off right. Looks front. Returns to up left center. Stands, facing downstage. Looks off right. Looks front.

First player begins again his entire sequence of movement.

At the point in the movement when the first player begins advancing upon the enemy, the third player extends his left arm to the side, then, moving the arm in an arc parallel to the floor, covers his eyes, at the same time extending all his fingers. He holds the cross more aloft.

As this is taking place, the second player puts on a small crown and holds a recorder (or flute). Second player crosses to center stage. Begins playing the recorder as the third player ceases movement.

The second player now darts and weaves between and around the other two players, playing the recorder, stopping to observe the other players from time to time, until the point in the movement when the first player crumples to the floor.

Second player crosses up center. Turns to face downstage. Continues playing until the first player ceases all movement, letting the final notes fall away.

Pause.

Second player returns up left center. Takes off crown. Puts down recorder and crown. Stands erect, facing downstage.

Simultaneously, the third player uncovers his eyes. Extends his left arm to the side, in reverse arc. He once again assumes the ecclesiastical pose. Returns cross to former position. Slowly lowers left arm to his side.

Pause.

Second player looks off right. Looks front. Crosses to first player. Helps him to his feet. Hands him his stick. Turns first player to face upstage. Second player stands facing downstage. Looks off right. Looks front.

Second player crosses to third player. Second player leads third player off left, second player again walks backwards. Second player re-enters alone. Crosses up left center, looking off right. Turns downstage, still looking off right. Looks front.

Looks off right. Looks front.

Pause.

Lights fade out completely.

End of "The Pawn, the Bishop, and the King."

Exercise in Five Acts

Bare stage.

Act One—Exposition

Lights up full.

Man and woman discovered standing approximately two feet apart. Woman is center stage. Man is to the right of the woman, right stage.

Pause.

The man lifts up his left hand from his side. Woman lifts up her right hand, until their hands meet. They now hold hands.

Pause.

Both players smile.

64

Pause.

Lights fade out (fast fade).

Act Two—Complication

Lights up full.

Man and woman discovered as at the end of Act One, holding hands and smiling.

Pause.

Second man enters from left. He crosses to the left of the woman. Faces front. Puts his arm around the waist of the woman.

Pause.

As the second man smiles, the woman expresses surprise, first man anger.

Pause.

Lights fade out (fast fade).

Act Three—Conflict

Lights up full.

The two men are now center stage, facing one another, approximately arm's length apart. The woman is upstage and between them, facing front.

Pause.

The first man (right stage) slowly forms a fist with his right hand. He extends his arm and fist in the direction of the face of the second man, without contact.

Pause.

Lights fade out (fast fade).

Act Four—Climax

Lights up full.

First man and woman are discovered in same positions as at the end of Act Three. Second man is flat on his back, parallel to the footlights, arms extended to the side. His eyes are closed.

Pause.

First man and woman look to second man.

Pause.

Lights fade out (fast fade).

Act Five—Resolution

Lights up full.

First man and woman are discovered in the same positions as at the beginning of Act One (woman center, man to her right).

Pause.

Man lifts up his left hand from his side. Woman brings up her right hand, until their hands meet. They now hold hands.

Pause.

Each player looks at the other. Both look front.

Pause.

Both players smile.

Pause.

Lights fade out (medium slow fade).

End of "Exercise in Five Acts."

Note: Some means of identifying each act for the audience may be necessary.

The Human Race

in three parts

One

Lights up full.

Bare stage.

First man enters, on the run, from right stage. Crosses to center, still running. Pauses at center, running. Exits left, running.

Pause.

First man enters from left, followed by second man, who is slightly upstage, both on the run. They cross to center, running. Pause at center, running. Exit right, running.

Pause.

First man enters from right stage, followed again by second man, slightly upstage, both running. They cross to center. Both stop running. They lean on one another for support, panting and coughing.

They both look off right. Both hastily commence running again. Exit left, running.

As they exit, woman enters from right, running in an exaggerated female style. She crosses to center, running. Pauses at center, running. Looks front with a rather silly expression. Exits left, still running.

Lights fade out.

Two

Lights up full.

Bare stage.

Two men enter from opposite sides of the stage, running. They cross to center until they are approximately two feet apart, facing each other, running.

They suddenly run into each other and fall to the floor in a heap, ceasing all movement.

Pause.

Both men suddenly jump up, continue running. Each takes an outside turn upstage, until they are once again facing each other, center stage, two feet apart, running.

Again they run into each other, fall to the floor, cease all movement.

Pause.

Again they jump up, take an outside turn downstage, until they are again facing each other, center, two feet apart, running.

Once again they run into each other, fall to the floor, cease all movement.

Pause.

Lights fade out.

Three

Lights up full.

First man discovered down center stage, facing left stage, walking. First man continues walking throughout the following:

Second man enters from right stage, slightly upstage of the first man, running. Second man slowly closes the gap between himself and the first man, and finally passes the first man, somewhat pleased with himself for his accomplishment.

The second man, still running forward, slowly begins moving backwards. He again passes the first man and, as he falls behind, tries desperately to catch up, but only succeeds in falling further behind, until he has completely exited off right, still running forward, moving backwards.

Pause.

First man now assumes an amused expression.

Lights fade out.

End of "The Human Race."

BIBLIOGRAPHY

Barlanghy, Istvan. *Mime: Training and Exercises.* New Rochelle, N.Y.: Sportshelf, 1967. Dance-oriented approach to mime in exercises. Little practical application of the material discussed in the book is given. Insight into character study and approach to the art is basically good.

Decroux, Étienne. *Paroles sur le Mime.* Paris: Editions d'art et Industrie, 1925.

Dorcy, Jean. *The Mime.* New York: Robert Speller and Sons, 1961. Includes essays by Decroux, Barrault, and Marceau, and photographs of same.

Enters, Angna. *On Mime.* Middleton, Conn.: Wesleyan University Press, 1965. Angna Enters on Angna Enters.

Humphrey, Doris. *The Art of Making Dances.* New York: Grove Press, 1959. Chapters on theme, motivation, and gesture in particular.

Hunt, Douglas and Kari. *Pantomime: The Silent Theatre.* New York: Atheneum, 1964. General history of pantomime and other tangent material.

von Pawlikowski-Cholewa, Harald. *Marcel Marceau.* Hamburg: Johannes-Maria Hoeppner, 1955. Book of photographs of Marceau.

Walker, Katherine Sorley. *Eyes on Mime.* New York: John Day Company, 1969. General history and discussion of "mime," only as it relates to ballet and dance. Very little material applicable to serious study. Photographs of various performers, solo and ensemble. Also contains a filmography, the bulk of which does not pertain to "mime."

FILMOGRAPHY

Les Enfants du Paradis—France, 1964. Jean-Louis Barrault as Deburau, a famous mime most identified with Pierrot.

Marcel Marceau

Royaumont—France, 1948.

Mic-Mac—France, 1949.

Paris-Montemartre—France, 1950. With Edith Piaf.

Pantomimes: Marcel Marceau—France, 1954. Includes "David and Goliath," "The Butterfly Chase," and "The Lion Tamer."

The Overcoat—Germany, 1955. Performed by *Compagnie de Mime Marcel Marceau.*

In the Park—France, 1956.

The Dinner Party—Germany, 1958.

Marcel Marceau or L'Art du Mime—France, 1965.

David Alberts

The Art of Silence—series includes illusory walking (side and front), climbing stairs, pulling a rope, skating, bicycle, walking against the wind. 1970.

Pantomimes—includes "Old Friends," "The Marionette," "The First Snow." 1970.

Mimes—includes "The Human Race," "The Pawn, the Bishop, and the King," "Mime for Three Players." Performed by Toronto Mime Ensemble. 1970.